Search Engine Optimization and Placement:

An Internet Marketing Course for Webmasters

Reneé Kennedy
Terry Kent

The Write Market

Search Engine Optimization and Placement:
An Internet Marketing Course for Webmasters

Reneé Kennedy
Terry Kent

The Write Market
rr1 Box 130M
Shenandoah Junction, WV 25442

www.upublish.com/books/kennedy.htm

http://www.thewritemarket.com

http://www.allwritedesign.com

Universal Publishers / uPUBLISH.com
USA • 2001

Written by: Reneé Kennedy
Designed by: Terry Kent

Notice of Rights

Notice of Liability

ISBN 1-58112-680-8

TABLE OF CONTENTS

INTRODUCTION

Successful search engine (SE) optimization requires strong organization, and this booklet, written for amateur optimizers, takes such organization to a new level. You must, however, have the ability to change text, meta tags, and title of your web pages.

We've provided space throughout this journal for you to jot down specifics so you can track what you've done and see what you have left to do.

We will frequently refer you to the Search Engine Promotion Tutorial located on the Internet (from now on referred to as the Online Tutorial). The Online Tutorial offers some of the same information given on these pages, however, it also has links to important articles and research that provide advanced information. It's regularly updated.

This publication, when combined with the Online Tutorial, gives you an excellent starting point. Use both tools to learn the basics before you branch off to more advanced techniques.

The link to the Online Tutorial is:

www.thewritemarket.com/intro.shtml

Because of the ways search engines and directories change their affiliations and their algorithms, we cannot list the majors in this booklet. For this you will need the Online Tutorial. We will, however, furnish you with the space needed to list the majors and keep track of their changes.

This book focuses on writing for the search engines an directories. However, we must also be aware of the people that we are writing for. The next section is about your visitors. If your web site's purpose is to sell a product or service then your visitors are also your "target market." The following section will give you specific strategies to help you sell a product or service.

BEFORE YOU BEGIN

Before you attempt to optimize, try to complete the following:

1. **Acquire your own domain name.** Search engines, and especially directories, are more likely to index the root domain than subdirectories of free sites. *Having your own domain name is imperative.*
2. **Achieve professional, attractive design.** Once you submit to directories, people will visit your site and decide its worth.
3. **Ensure that your site has proper navigation.** This allows search engines to follow your links, just as real people will do when visiting your site. Sometimes, organization is what distinguishes one site from another.
4. **Write and develop your content.** *Content is King.* All search engines, directories, or otherwise, will index your web site based on CONTENT. ALL of them. This is the KEY to getting your site well known around the Internet.
    a. Build a good reputation with high-quality content.
    b. Offer specific content to attract visitors. Find a niche and stick to it. Become one of the best sites in your niche by providing specific, original content.
    c. Other sites will link to your site if you have original content.

The purpose of this booklet is to help you write your content in ways that both people and search engines can understand.

WRITING STRATEGIES

1. **Write in "chunks."** Don't overwhelm visitors with too much information in one paragraph. Keep your paragraphs at two to three sentences each.
2. **Use headings.** Headings make your pages easily scannable.
3. **Use lists.** Lists create scannability, as well.
4. **Bold.** Bolding is best used to highlight important information. Bolding is also effective in search engine promotion (bolding keywords, for example).
5. **Write at an eighth grade reading level.** You want to make a web page easy to read. That doesn't mean that it shouldn't be interesting. While you need to keep your visitors excited about your content, many people don't have time to read involved text. If you need to include detailed explanations, save them for other pages: your first priority is getting visitors interested. Which sentence is easier to read?
   a. Keep your words and phrases short, or your visitors may leave your site.
   b. Using convoluted explanations of your products or services may disorient your visitors. This confusion may cause your visitors to go elsewhere.

6. **Write it the way you say it.** Don't write it as if you were writing a textbook. Do write conversationally.

   Talk to yourself! Having trouble getting something on paper? Dictate, using a tape recorder. Verbalize what you want to say on your web page into the tape recorder - then transfer that to the web page.
7. **Focus on your target.** Once you have figured out who your targets are, focus your writing on them. Write just for them. For instance, if you are targeting webmasters, your writing may include words that webmasters understand - words like "server," "host," and "FTP."

If, however, you are targeting people with no knowledge of the web, seriously think about your language. If you are writing to housewives, use their lingo and discuss benefits they would understand and relate to.

8. **Focus on the individual.** Write to an individual, not to a group of people. Use the word "you," e.g., "Have you ever had time to sit down and read a book?" Avoid phrases like, "Many people never have time to sit down and read a book." Make it personal.

9. **Use spacing and punctuation marks and symbols to their fullest advantage** (- . , ! " % $ & ~ : to name a few). The dash (—) can be very powerful – leading people to the next bit of text. Get a little creative.

10. **Write then rewrite, edit, rewrite, edit, and rewrite**...it's an endless process. Never let your writing rest; there is always something you can improve.

NAVIGATION STRATEGIES

Navigation will be made up of three different strategies:

1. Web Copy
2. Navigational Structure
3. Graphics and Navigational Directory

WEB COPY:

Your web copy needs to *lead* your customers to the sale. It needs to pull them down the page, forcing them to scroll, because they want to read what comes next. And at the bottom, it must make them want to click to the next page.

Before you begin to think about your navigational structure, try to have a good idea of what you are going to say on your web pages. You also need a goal or purpose for each page.

The navigational structure will be developed as you write your web copy.

NAVIGATIONAL STRUCTURE:

Here is an outline of a very simple navigational structure for one product:

1. Opening Page or Home - emphasis on benefits
2. Secondary Page(s) or Features - features and pictures of the product
3. Testimonials
4. Guarantee and/or Warranty
5. Closing Page or Order - Ask for the Sale (This is where you want to include the prices.)

If you are trying to sell more than one product with your site:

1. Consider a maximum of 8 links in your "main" directory.
2. If you have more than 8 pages, then use sub-directories.
3. Avoid going beyond third level sub-directories.

GRAPHICS AND NAVIGATIONAL DIRECTORY:

Your navigational directory or navigational bar may be placed at the top and bottom of all your pages, or on the left-hand side of your pages. Your navigational bar may be made from graphics or text links. You don't *need* graphics, but if you choose to use them, make sure they look professional!

We recommend placing the navigational directory on the left-hand side of the web page for two reasons:

1. People are used to having the directory on the left-hand side.
2. Right-aligning directories can cause problems in older versions of some browsers.

Your navigational bar at the top and bottom of your pages, might look like this:

Home | Features | Testimonials | Guarantee | Order Now

In every section that offers a product or requires a response, always offer a link to the target response. For example, "Order Now," or "Free Consultation."

TIPS:

Tips:

1. Layout the flow of your site on paper before attempting to put it on the web.
2. Write your web copy first. At least, have a general feeling of what it will say before you attempt a navigational structure.
3. Continually go back and re-examine your navigation - as your site gets bigger think about clearly outlining the purpose of the site on the home page.
4. Don't underline any text that is not a link.
5. Understand that as search engines begin to index your pages - people may end up coming into your site from various pages - not necessarily your homepage. Can people still find their way around if they come into your site from any page? Do people still understand the purpose of your site if they come in from any page?
6. Make sure you have links to and from your home page or wherever you keep your "main directory" on every page of your site. This will also help the search engine spiders find their way around.

GENERAL SEARCH ENGINE INFORMATION

Search Engines are one of the ways surfers find products, services and information on the Web. In order for a site to get the most exposure on the Web, it is essential that the site is listed in the major search engines and directories. One advantage for small business sites is that there are only a few major engines and directories. The minor ones will take their data from the majors. This section will explain how the engines work.

SEARCH ENGINE TERMS

Search Engine: A server that indexes web sites. A search engine is a machine *tuned* by humans to rank web pages. AltaVista is an example of a search engine.

Algorithm: The way in which the search engine is *tuned*. An algorithm is the way the search engine is programmed to determine ranks.

Directory: A list of sites compiled by humans. Yahoo is an example of a directory.

Spider: A spider *crawls* your site and finds your pages. It then stores those pages in a database for later retrieval by a search engine when someone queries the search engine.

Indexing: Occurs when the search engine takes the pages from the database the spider has created and places them in an order based on the algorithms of that engine. All search engines have different indexing processes because they have different algorithms. That's why you get different results in various engines.

Query: The keywords a person types into a search box. The person is *querying* the search engine.

Crawling: When the spider follows the links from the page you submit - the spider is *crawling* your site.

Optimization: Making changes to a web site in order to increase ranks in a search engine.

Examples of spam:

a. Using the same word or phrase several times in your title, meta tags or text

b. Putting words or phrases into your meta tags or title that have nothing to do with the actual content people see on your web page

c. Using text, spacers, or borders the same color as the background

d. Using tiny text with keywords in an attempt to increase ranks

SEARCH ENGINES V. DIRECTORIES

There is a difference between a search engine and a directory. A search engine is a machine - or a *robot.* A human may program algorithms for a search engine, but a human has nothing to do with your site when the spider is visiting your site or when the engine is indexing your pages.

A robot may compile a directory, but humans compile the major directories. Yahoo is a prime example of a directory. When you submit your site to Yahoo, a human will review your site for consideration in the Yahoo index.

Each major *search engine* is usually associated with a *directory.* For instance, when you go to AltaVista and you type in a search, you are definitely getting results from the engine part of AltaVista. But when you search through its categories (you haven't typed anything into the search box), you get results from a directory. These results come from the LookSmart directory, which AltaVista is using as we go to press.

There is a relationship between search results in the engine and the directory or directories that are associated with a particular search engine. It appears that many search engines' algorithms have been programmed to include results based on their directories. *Therefore, if you are trying to increase your ranks in a particular search engine, then it is imperative that you are listed in the directory associated with that search engine.*

SEARCH ENGINE RELATIONSHIPS

They're all related. Each search engine and directory will use results from other search engines or directories. Please go to the Online Tutorial if you'd like to know the exact nature of these relationships. (They tend to change regularly.)

Is it important that you know all of the affiliations? Not really. You can still optimize and submit your pages to the search engines and you can submit your home page to every directory, and not be penalized. In fact, it will help if you submit your site to individual search engines and directories.

Why do they all interrelate? Because every search site wants to have the freshest data on the Net. Some of them compete for the biggest index of sites on the Net. If they draw from different sources, it helps them maintain a fresh database and a large one. However, just because two engines both take information from the same database does not mean that they rank that information in the same way.

Also, it is a safe assumption that surfers will find a particular search engine and stick with it. They learn how to use it; they become familiar with it. The interrelations between search engines and directories do not matter to the average surfer. The average surfer wants fresh content.

It is also possible that a surfer would like to go to an engine and get different content every time. AltaVista has been known to rotate algorithms. This means that today you may type in a keyword and bring up a specific set of web sites, then (perhaps the following day), you type in the same keyword and bring up a totally different set of results.

You cannot worry about what the search engines are doing. It is more to your advantage to create content-rich pages that focus on one or two particular keywords and submit these pages to each search engine.

WHAT HAPPENS WHEN I SUBMIT A URL TO A SEARCH ENGINE?

First, the search engine's spider visits your site immediately, and schedules your site for inclusion in the search engine's index.

Second, usually within a few weeks, the engine places your site in its index.

Third, the spider revisits (automatically updates) your site to include changes you've made on each page listed in the index. Once the page is in the index, the spider usually revisits every two weeks. The spider will also begin to "crawl" your site by following the links from the page you submitted. This is why your navigation structure is so important.

Fourth, when people use a search engine, they type keywords into a search box. They are submitting a query. The search engine, depending on algorithms, will pull up all of the sites relevant to that query.

WHAT IF I DON'T WANT A PAGE INDEXED?

If you want to prevent a search engine from indexing certain pages, use the following tag on these pages: <meta name="robots" content="noindex">.

Better yet, simply include a robots.txt file in your main directory - you can exclude all engines from certain parts of your site, or specific engines from specific pages. Directions on how to do this are located in the Online Tutorial.

VARIABLES THAT AFFECT RANKS

When you are optimizing your web pages, be aware that your writing is the most important part of how a search engine ranks your pages. ALL search engines rank pages based on the visible words on a web page.

Some engines also contain algorithms to give a boost to pages that meet the following criteria (all of these criteria will be discussed in more detail throughout this booklet):

1. Percentage of keywords in the visible text (keyword density)
2. Link popularity
3. Click popularity
4. Keywords in the title
5. Keywords in the description tag
6. Keywords in the keywords tag
7. Keywords in the names of linked pages and in the linked words, for instance, <a href="wooden-boats">wooden boats</a>
8. Keywords in alt tags
9. Keywords as names of images, for instance, <img src="wooden-boats.gif" alt="wooden boats">
10. Paying for ranks
11. Listing in online directories

POPULARITY

Link popularity and/or click popularity are determined separately by each search engine. AltaVista may calculate a high popularity for your site, whereas Lycos may calculate a low popularity for your site. Each search engine may also use the popularity information in different ways. It depends on their specific algorithms.

Popularity is becoming more widely used by search engines.

Therefore, it is a very important consideration when trying to increase your ranks. Hypothetically, if you have two sites that have equal content and equal meta tags, then the site with more popularity will rank higher.

Link Popularity:

1. The link popularity of your site is determined by:
    a. The number of web sites linking to your site (the web page on which your link appears must be indexed by the search engine; "free-for-all-links-pages" are not the kind of links that you're looking for)
    b. The popularity of those sites linking to your site
    c. The similarity of the content on sites that link to your site
2. Every search engine to some extent uses link popularity.

Click popularity:

1. Click popularity is the number of clicks your site gets when it comes up in a search. So if your site is Number 3 for a search, and it is being clicked on by people more than Number 2, you can potentially move ahead of Number 2 (if the engine uses click popularity in its algorithms).
2. Direct Hit is the main engine that uses click popularity. Engines associated with Direct Hit indirectly use click popularity.

Find out who's linking to you:

There is information in the Online Tutorial on how to discover your link popularity with several search engines. There are also several tools available to check your link popularity.

HOW TO INCREASE POPULARITY

Reciprocal Links:

Consider a reciprocal linking campaign. However, you must offer links to other sites in a judicious manner.

Two considerations:

1. Don't link off your site from your home page.
2. Provide content other than just links to other sites.

The Write Market started with a one-page resource directory. From there, it was built to over 10 pages of links that go to sites with content similar to its own. We started by simply linking to anything related to us. Now we are fussy. We will only link to a site that will give us a reciprocal link, and we only link to sites with quality content.

It's a lot of work to maintain even a small reciprocal link directory, so you will need to have time to commit to it.

Content:

CONTENT IS KING. No one wants to link to a site that is simply a promotional avenue for an affiliate program. You must provide original content. If you offer original content, you'll find sites linking to you from all over the Internet.

Online Directories:

Getting listings in directories will not only boost your traffic, it will also increase your link popularity. It is especially relevant to link popularity because these directories are mega popular (the more popular a site is that links to you, the higher in popularity your site will be rated). This booklet will discuss how to get into the major directories.

Title and Description:

You will be able to increase your click popularity by having a good title and description of your web site. More information on the title and description will follow.

WRITING FOR SEARCH ENGINE PROMOTION

Search engine promotion is all about the words on a page. The following sections will give you step-by-step strategies to improve your writing.

BRAINSTORMING

Brainstorming involves choosing a subject, then opening your mind and writing down anything that comes into your head. If you brainstorm with a group of people, you get more ideas than when doing it by yourself.

Use brainstorming for finding keywords, creating titles, writing headlines, descriptions, and other types of content for your pages.

Process:

1. Gather a group of people - five is a good number.
2. Generally discuss the topic. We'll use keywords as our example. Those gathered in the room will need to know what keywords are. Answer any questions people might have before you begin. The person in charge might then say, "We're here to brainstorm keywords for a web page that sells educational toys. When I say, 'go,' I want everyone to start calling out any word or phrase that comes

into their minds in relation to this web page. The phrase can be as long or as short as you want."

3. It's best if you have a chalkboard, an erasable marker board, or large sheets of paper tacked to the wall.
4. Have two people responsible for writing down the called-out words.
5. The rest of the group is responsible for calling out ideas.
6. That's it! Have the members call out anything that comes to mind - it can be noisy, fun, and very revealing!

What if I don't have a big group of people?

If you are doing this alone, we recommend talking to other people about what you came up with. A second and third opinion can be extremely helpful. Maybe have a mini-brainstorming session with individuals willing to take a few minutes to sit down with you.

You *can* do this on your own. Just remember not to worry about spelling, grammar, punctuation or any conventions - the whole idea of brainstorming is to let your ideas flow without restrictions. You can take time, later on, to adhere to the conventions of the English language. Brainstorming is for getting the ideas out - it gets them from your mind onto paper.

Keep a record:

When you come up with a list of ideas or words, keep them on hand. You will be able to refer back to them when you get stuck for a word or a phrase. Save your ideas, but try to keep them organized and in a notebook. Put some kind of title on the pages so you will be able to quickly find what you're looking for. For instance, we might title the above process: "Keywords for educational toys."

BEGIN TO WRITE CONTENT

We've already stated that your content is the most important part of search engine promotion. However, your first step is to get your ideas on the web page.

1. Go to your web page and put in some content. Get your main ideas down. Ask yourself some questions:
    * What is the goal of promoting this page?
    * What do I want to get out of this page?
    * Who do I want to come to this page?
    * What would those people want to read?
2. Organize it. Use an outline, use headers and lists. It doesn't have to stay in those forms, but using them will help keep you focused.
3. Write about 200-300 words on the page.
4. If you're having trouble getting something on the page, try writing it as if you were explaining it to someone. Pretend you're talking to someone and put those words on your page. Try to brainstorm...just let your ideas flow...you can fix the details later.
5. This is a rough draft. Don't expend a lot of energy making it sound wonderful. You are going to have to rewrite it several times, anyway.

META TAGS

Use Meta Tags to help improve your rankings and also to help SEs index your pages. However, when you start looking at specific search engines, you will notice that not all SEs support meta tags. When you start analyzing your competitors' sites, you will find that some pages ranking in the top 10 do not use meta tags. Nevertheless, in order to do the most thorough job of promoting, use meta tags.

Here is how the placement of your meta tags should look:

```
<HTML>
<HEAD>
<TITLE>my page</TITLE>
<META NAME="DESCRIPTION" CONTENT="description of my site.">
<META NAME="KEYWORDS" CONTENT="my keywords">
</HEAD>
```

More resources on meta tags are available in the Online Tutorial.

Following the explanations of Keywords, Description, and Title, you will find several pages designed for you to write down your tags.

KEYWORD TERMS

Keyword: A word that people type into a search engine in order to find web sites that relate to that word. A query.

Keyword Phrase: Two or three words in a string. Some examples: "educational toys," "children's books," "wooden boats." Generally, a noun (person, place, or thing) and one or two adjectives (words that describe nouns).

Keyword Proximity: When two or three keywords are placed together, and how close they are to each other. For instance: "educational books" v. "educational children's books" v. "educational children's monster books." You want words to be placed together when you think people might type them into a search engine exactly that way - a keyword phrase.

Keyword Frequency: (Also termed *Keyword Density*) The amount of times a keyword or keyword phrase appears in the text of a web page (can also include the keyword in the title, meta tags, and alt tags.) This is usually referred to as a percentage.

Keyword/Total Words in Text=3% or

Keyword/Total Words in Text, Title and Tags=5%

Stemming: You will notice that when you type a plural into some search engines, like "toys," the engine will change it to the singular, "toy." This is because the engine will read only the root of the word. The term for this is called *stemming*. Generally, use the version of the word that you feel people would use in a query. Stick with that version throughout your text, title, and tags.

Stop words: You may notice that some search engines do not use words like these in a search: *a, and, the, of, that, it,* and *to.*

FIND KEYWORDS

Before you begin to rewrite the content of your web page to increase or decrease keyword frequency, you must find the *right* keywords. There are several ways to go about this:

1. **Brainstorm.** Come up with at least 10 keywords or keyword phrases that you think people might type into a search engine in order to find your web page. Keep a list of these words in this booklet. (You'll find pages in the booklet where you may write them down.) Be sure to label each keyword with the appropriate pages that they belong on. Keep adding to your list when you find new words. This will become a useful resource for your web site.
2. **Ask business people and friends** what they would type into a search if they were looking for your page or site.
3. **Go to search engines** and look for pages with content similar to your own. Look at their source code. Check out which phrases they are using in their keyword meta tags. However, do not copy someone else's words or their pages. This is stealing/plagiarism and can be punished on the Internet as severely as in real time.
4. Run your keywords through the **"GoTo Suggestion" tool.** Link available in Online Tutorial. You may have to sign up for GoTo ($25) in order to get this tool to work. However, it is an eye opener and will be useful in helping you narrow your keyword choices. There are a few other free tools available for keyword searching in the Online Tutorial.
5. **Target your keywords.** If you pick a general (common) word that is highly searched, you are less likely to get a good ranking than if

you pick a phrase that is less highly searched but more specific. For example, the keyword "toy" is too general. What kind of toys are we trying to promote? If we narrow it down to "educational toy" or "wooden toy," we have a better chance of getting a good rank ("good rank" meaning in the top ten).

You also reach fewer people this way. Therefore, try for the highly searched words, but also have some phrases that are less highly searched.

Getting very specific is important, not only for rankings, but also because you want people to find what you are offering. You don't want people to be annoyed when they get to your page because they were looking for something else.

Example: These are the keywords we will use for the rest of our example page:

educational

wooden

toys

boats

educational toys

wooden boats

educational wooden boats

KEYWORDS

Words	Web Page
wooden boats	wooden-boats.htm

KEYWORDS

Words	Web Page

KEYWORDS

Words	Web Page

KEYWORDS

Words	Web Page

WRITE THE KEYWORDS TAG

Suggestions for writing your keywords tag:

1. Try not to use an individual word more than three times. This includes all forms (derivatives) of it. For example, "childrens" and "children's" might be considered the same word by some engines because of stemming. It would be prudent to pick one of these words and stick with it on a particular page, then if you must account for the other word, use it on another page.
2. Use keyword phrases to the best of your ability.
3. Try to limit your character count to 1,000.
4. Use the most important keywords or keyword phrases first.
5. Should you separate your keywords with commas? There is evidence that using commas limits your phrases to those words within the commas. If you choose not to use commas, you might open your page to more keyword phrases. For instance, if your tag is "educational toys wooden boats," you might get ranked for "educational wooden boats," but if the tag reads "educational toys, wooden boats," you'd have less of a chance to get ranked for "educational wooden boats" because the comma separates the words.

Example:

<META NAME="KEYWORDS" CONTENT="wooden boats, educational toys, educational wooden toys, wooden toys, boats, educational">

WRITE THE TITLE

Titles are the links that you see in the SEs when you perform searches. SEs generally have about 10 titles per search. Under each title, you will see a description of the site.

Those titles that you see are generated directly from the <TITLE> tag in a web page. *It is extremely important to have a title on every page you want to promote in search engines.* In fact, there is evidence that a title is one of the most important factors affecting search engine ranks.

Write the title carefully. Not only must you use keywords, you must also make it interesting. Here are some guidelines:

1. Look at your keywords and keyword phrases.
2. In your title, include as many of the words from your keywords and keyword phrases as possible. Try to use each word only once. Think about stemming.
3. Making the title catchy might be difficult, but try it anyway. The title is the first thing everyone sees that describes your site. You want people to look further (the description is next) so the title has to grab them. Here are some tips:
    a. Ask a question
    b. Solve a problem
    c. Solve a problem quickly: time
    d. Solve a problem for a cheap price: money
4. The first words you use in the title are the most important words to the SE, so use your most important keyword phrases as near the beginning of the title as possible.
5. Most people use lower case letters to search, and some engines are case specific.
6. Don't use all caps: they are difficult to read. Make your title a sentence if you can, capitalizing only the first word.
7. Try to keep the title to within 100 characters. Characters include spaces, punctuation and letters.

Examples:

<TITLE>Educational toys including wooden boats!</TITLE>

<TITLE>Wooden boats make educational toys: buy online!</TITLE>

<TITLE>Educational toys, discounts on wooden boats. Overnight delivery!</TITLE>

WRITE THE DESCRIPTION

Not every search engine uses the description tag. But because it is used by most of them, it is beneficial to have it on your page.

Here are some guidelines for writing the description:

1. Think about these two questions:
   a. What is this page about?
   b. Who is the target of this page? In other words, who do you want to come to your page?
2. Make your description simple and to the point. Lure them to your page. Use keywords if you can, but make it sound exciting! Explain what makes your site unique. If you can throw in a word like "free," "discounts," or "resources," do it here. Also, if you can solve their problems quickly, say so. People are always looking for bargains and quick solutions.
3. Try to limit character count to 150.
4. Put your most important info first, because some engines will cut off the description after the first 150 characters.

Example:

<META NAME="DESCRIPTION" CONTENT="Offering educational toys, wooden boats and puzzles. Free letter from Santa with purchase of two or more toys! Online ordering and overnight delivery.">

Keywords and Meta Tags

Page: ____________ **Date:** ____________

Possible Keywords:

Title:

Description Meta Tag:

Keywords Meta Tag:

Keywords and Meta Tags

Page: ____________________ **Date:** ________________________

Possible Keywords:

____

____

____

____

____

Title:

____

____

____

____

____

Description Meta Tag:

____

____

____

____

____

Keywords Meta Tag:

____

____

____

____

____

Keywords and Meta Tags

Page: ____________________ **Date:** ______________________

Possible Keywords:

____

____

____

____

____

Title:

____

____

____

____

____

Description Meta Tag:

____

____

____

____

____

Keywords Meta Tag:

____

____

____

____

____

Keywords and Meta Tags

Page: ____________________ **Date:** ______________________

Possible Keywords:

Title:

Description Meta Tag:

Keywords Meta Tag:

Keywords and Meta Tags

Page: ____________________ **Date:** ______________________

Possible Keywords:

____

____

____

____

____

Title:

____

____

____

____

____

Description Meta Tag:

____

____

____

____

____

Keywords Meta Tag:

____

____

____

____

____

Keywords and Meta Tags

Page: ____________________ **Date:** ______________________

Possible Keywords:

Title:

Description Meta Tag:

Keywords Meta Tag:

Keywords and Meta Tags

Page: ____________________ **Date:** ______________________

Possible Keywords:

Title:

Description Meta Tag:

Keywords Meta Tag:

Keywords and Meta Tags

Page: ____________________ **Date:** ______________________

Possible Keywords:

____

____

____

____

____

Title:

____

____

____

____

____

Description Meta Tag:

____

____

____

____

____

Keywords Meta Tag:

____

____

____

____

____

REWRITE THE CONTENT

Rewriting is perhaps the hardest part. It is also the most important part. While some search engines use Meta Tags, all search engines use words in the text to rank pages. Some search engines rely mainly on keyword frequency in text to rank pages.

Tips:

1. Try for around 200-300 words per page.
2. Try to keep your paragraphs natural. Don't mass all your keywords together. Try to scatter them throughout your text.
3. Some SEs "read" alt tags. If you can't fit enough words in your text, put the extra ones into your alt tags.
4. Consider placing keywords in linked text.
5. Surround some of your important keywords with bold, strong, and heading tags. These tags will help the SEs find the words that you use them on.
6. Remember proximity. Try to keep important phrases together. For example, we might use "educational wooden boats" rather than "educational boats."
7. In general, try for a 3-4% density for your most important phrases or keywords. Each search engine will have its own algorithms regarding density. Usually 3-4% is safe for all engines. Some engines will allow you to use a higher frequency. You will want to run tests and experiment with the different engines. This booklet provides you with space to write and keep track of your notes on the search engines you choose to optimize for. Optimize specific pages for specific engines. In the Online Tutorial, you will find detailed information on each major search engine. There are also tools available in the Online Tutorial to help you calculate keyword density.
8. Check everything twice. After rewriting, go back and look at your text a second and possibly a third time.

SUBMITTING

This booklet will only cover hand submission. The most effective method of submitting is to go to each search engine and submit your main URLs directly to the engine. Most engines have made it easy to do this and it provides much more effective results than mass submission tools.

The Online Tutorial has an updated list of the engines that you should submit to. We provide links to the pages where you will submit your site. Submitting to these major search engines will also get you listed in the minor ones (which we don't list).

SUBMIT TO THE ENGINES

1. Generally, until you are in the index, submit your site once a month.
2. When you first submit your pages, submit all your important pages (see next item!).
3. Don't submit too many pages in one day - submit a few every day for a week.
4. Don't submit the same page twice to the same engine on the same day.
5. Once your page is indexed, don't resubmit it unless you've made changes to it.
6. Read everything provided on the page where you submit. Read about each engine's submission practices. It can vary from engine

to engine.

7. **Keep track!** Write down the following:

   * The engines you submitted to
   * The pages you submitted
   * The date you submitted them
   * The date you verified that the page was added to the index.

We have provided the following pages for you to write down this information. Each page should represent a different search engine. Use the notes area to write down different strategies for optimization for that particular engine. You will find some strategies in the Online Tutorial's Search Engine Specifics page.

Search Engine: ____________________

Day Submitted	Page Submitted	Day Verified
5-1-00	trains.htm	12-1-00

Notes: ____________________

Search Engine: ____________________

Day Submitted	Page Submitted	Day Verified

Notes: ____________________

Search Engine: ____________________

Day Submitted	Page Submitted	Day Verified

Notes: ____________________

Search Engine: ______________________

Day Submitted	Page Submitted	Day Verified

Notes: ______________________

Search Engine: ____________________

Day Submitted	Page Submitted	Day Verified

Notes: ____________________

Search Engine: ______________________

Day Submitted	Page Submitted	Day Verified

Notes: ____

Search Engine: ____________________

Day Submitted	Page Submitted	Day Verified

Notes: ____________________

Search Engine: ____________________

Day Submitted	Page Submitted	Day Verified

Notes: ____________________

Search Engine: ____________________

Day Submitted	Page Submitted	Day Verified

Notes: ____________________

Search Engine: ______________________

Day Submitted	Page Submitted	Day Verified

Notes: ____

Search Engine: ____________________

Day Submitted	Page Submitted	Day Verified

Notes: ____________________

SUBMIT TO THE DIRECTORIES

While there are many online directories, there are only about four that are truly important to your search engine positioning campaigns. *It is imperative that you get into the major directories if you are trying to increase your ranks in search engines.* At the URL immediately below, you will find links to each major online directory as well as specific information about submitting to each one:

www.thewritemarket.com/directories/directories.htm

Tips:

1. Do not submit more than once. These directories know when you've submitted more than once and they will consider you a spammer if you continue to submit the same site over and over OR if you submit to several different categories.
2. Drill down through the categories before choosing one or two categories to submit to. Spend a few hours surfing the directory. This point cannot be stressed enough: *become familiar with the directory before you submit.*
3. Write a brief one- or two-line summary of your web site. If they ask for 25 words or less, give them 25 words or less. Do not try to cram all your keywords into the description. Do try to include a few of your main keywords.
4. The home page is the easiest page to get accepted. Consider submitting subdirectories if they have a lot of content on a particular theme.
5. Problems: unfortunately, these human-edited directories can be problematic. Study the tips we provide in the Online Tutorial for each directory, and read (until you fully understand) each separate directory's submission guidelines. Chances are, if you are not getting a listing, it is because you did not follow the guidelines. If it is because of human error, then you have the right to appeal, but appeal politely.

6. Keep track of the dates when you submitted to each directory, and go back later to verify your listings. This booklet provides the following pages for you to keep track of your submissions to the Online Directories.

Directory: ______________________

Day Submitted	Pg. Submitted	Category	Day Verified
5-11-00	index.htm	educational toys	8-9-00

Notes: ______________________

Directory: ______________________

Day Submitted	Pg. Submitted	Category	Day Verified

Notes: ______________________

Directory: ______________________

Day Submitted	Pg. Submitted	Category	Day Verified

Notes: ____

Directory: ______________________

Day Submitted	Pg. Submitted	Category	Day Verified

Notes: ______________________

Directory: ______________________

Day Submitted	Pg. Submitted	Category	Day Verified

Notes: ______________________

ANALYSIS

In order to find out if your ranks and listings are improving your traffic or your sales you will need to know:

1. How many unique visitors you get each week
2. Which search engines are sending you traffic
3. How many hits each search engine is sending you
4. Which keywords people use to find your site
5. What your ranks are for certain keywords
6. Sales/week

TRACK VISITORS AND RANKS

Track Visitors:

A *unique visitor* is one person who has visited your site. When you start to analyze the data, you will see a lot of numbers. Make sure that you are not getting the *total hits* on your site. Total hits can be anything from hits on every page to hits on every page and every graphic (total accesses). You need *number of unique visitors.*

In order to figure out how many unique visitors you get each week and also some of the other information in the list above, you need some way to track your traffic.

The cheapest route is to find a host that also provides a *usage log.* Also, be sure that you request *referrer logs.* These logs will provide you with a lot of information on how much traffic you are getting. It breaks down that information by page. It will also provide you with a general idea of where some of this traffic comes from. However, usage and referrer logs will not give you information about search engines in an easy-to-understand format.

We recommend that you find a tool that will organize the information in a way you can easily understand. There is a list of some of those tools in the Online Tutorial in the section called "Track Visitors." Some are free, and some you pay for.

Track Ranks:

First, you need to see if your web page is in a search engine.

You can usually find your web page by typing the URL into the search box. If you can't find it in this manner, try typing in a keyword phrase that would appear on your web page.

Then, if you are in the search engine, you need to see where you rank for specific keywords. You can go to each search engine and type in your keywords and see where you end up in the listing. Write down your ranks and track them over time to see if your optimization efforts are improving your ranks.

There is also a list of tools available to find your web page and track ranks in the Online Tutorial in the section called "Track Ranks."

ANALYZE TRAFFIC

Before you start to analyze, consider:

1. Logs and tools are not going to be perfectly accurate because of the nature of domains, servers, hosts, browsers, etc. However, these numbers are useful in giving you a general idea of trends in your traffic over a period of time. A tool that places code directly on each web page is the most accurate.
2. Determine your goals in a SE promotion campaign. Is it to increase traffic, increase sales, or create sales leads?
3. Don't expect to get every page ranked in every engine.

4. When you start getting a good amount of traffic (500 *uniques* a week) you will start to understand that the keyword phrases people type into the engines are wide and varied. If you optimize for many keywords (say 10 phrases), you will notice that you're getting traffic from search engines on phrases that you never thought of. The essence of a good SE promotion campaign is that you see a nice spread of traffic from ALL engines and directories and that you see a nice spread of keywords.
5. A promotion campaign for search engines (and directories) can be any of the following:
    * Getting a listing in a directory
    * Getting a good rank for a specific keyword in a specific search engine
    * A full-scale campaign to increase ranks in all major search engines and/or directories

Generally, you will see an increase in a comprehensive campaign over a period of weeks. For more specific campaigns, you may see an immediate increase (especially campaigns involving directories).

The simplest way to analyze traffic is to use the following equations (please note that this method is not statistical analysis, it is only a simple way to help you determine if your campaign is working):

Percent Increase of Unique Visitors:

UVB = unique visitors before a promotion campaign. They should be over a specific period of time, like 4 weeks.

UVA = unique visitors after a promotion campaign. This should be over the same period of time as UVB - 4 weeks.

UVA - UVB = difference

Difference/UVA = percent of visitor increase

Percent Increase of Hits from Search Engine(s):

HB = hits from search engine(s) before a campaign over specific time

HA = hits from search engines after a campaign over same time period as HB

HA - HB = difference

Difference/HA = percent increase of hits from search engine(s)

Percent increase in sales:

On the same day of each week (or month) you should calculate your sales/unique visitor ratio. This will tell you if your promotion campaigns are increasing sales, not just visitors. (We'll venture to say that 1% is a good ratio. That is one sale per 100 visitors. If you see anything over 1%, you should examine the campaign and try to replicate it in any way possible.)

Sales/Unique Visitors = percent of sales/visitors

REAL LIFE EXAMPLE

We wanted to figure out if getting a listing on Yahoo generated any increase in traffic, and if so, the approximate percentage of increase.

First, we generated the following data:

Unique visitors before listing/ 4 weeks = 5589

Unique visitors after listing/ 4 weeks = 7263

Then we used the following equations:

7263 - 5589 = 1674

What percent of 7263 = 1674?

1674 / 7263 = .23 or 23%

We determined that there was approximately a 23% increase in traffic after the listing in Yahoo. Which doesn't necessarily mean it was because of the Yahoo listing.

We also wanted to figure out more accurately the percentage of search engine/directory traffic that Yahoo was now accounting for.

2006 = total hits from search engines/directories before listing

2883 = total hits after listing

568 = total hits only from Yahoo listing

What percent of 2883 = 568?

568 / 2883 = approximately .20 = 20%

Now, since we were not doing any other search engine promotion during the four weeks prior to the Yahoo listing and the four weeks after the Yahoo listing, we also estimated that the Yahoo listing was affecting our ranks in other search engines. This can be true because many of the search engines will collect links from the directories. We wanted to know:

2883 - 2006 = 877

What percent of 2883 = 877?

877 / 2883 = 30%

What do all these percentages tell us? The Yahoo listing has increased our traffic APPROXIMATELY 20-30%.

WHAT IF THERE IS NO INCREASE IN TRAFFIC?

What if you optimized and gathered your data and found that your optimization did not improve your traffic?

1. Are you even in the search engines? Meaning, are you in the databases? It is important to be in all databases. See Track Ranks.
2. If you are in the engines, you may need to rewrite your pages. See Rewrite Content.
3. Examine your keywords to see if you have a nice spread of words bringing hits throughout all engines. Do those words accurately reflect your site? See Keywords.
4. Think about link popularity. See Popularity.
5. Analyze your high-ranking competition. Analyze their keyword den-

sity, meta tags, titles, and popularity. (There are several tools available in the Online Tutorial that will help you do this.) Try to emulate your high-ranking competition, but do not plagiarize.

OTHER SEARCH ENGINE POSITIONING TECHNIQUES

THEMES

Your site may be themed if your web pages surround a basic idea, motif, notion, or concept - however you choose to say it. You may have 10 or more keywords or keyword phrases that relate to your theme. For instance - "children," "books," "children's books," "books for children," "child," "kids," "juvenile books"- could build to the theme "children's books." When building your web site, *always keep your theme in mind* and build around that theme using keywords for each page that enhance and support the theme.

Alta Vista is rumored to use themes to rank pages. For more information on how to develop a theme based web site, go to the Online Tutorial on the page "Themes."

DOORWAYS

Doorway pages are also termed "hallway pages," "gateway pages," "entry pages," "leader pages," and "bridge pages."

They are "entrances" into your web site: web pages specifically written for a certain search engine. For instance, many people use doorway pages to get their sites into Alta Vista. They create separate pages with specific words and tags in them, expressly designed for Alta Vista.

Other things that may qualify a doorway page:

1. A page with a string of keywords - a list of keywords - no true, recognizable content.
2. Pages hosted on a server that is not where your web site is located. These pages are optimized to get ranks in the search engines, which then direct people to your web site. (Generally, a Search Engine Optimization Specialist might host your pages on his/her server.)
3. Pages that may be located on the same domain as your web site. They will lead people from a search engine to your home page.
4. A page that is optimized for specific keywords - with recognizable content in complete sentences. (This is what this booklet teaches you to do.)

For more information on Doorway Pages, please see the Online Tutorial.

PAYING FOR RANKS, LISTINGS, OR SPIDERING

At some point, you will want to consider paying money in order to get into engines and directories. It's just plain easier. You will have to weigh the cost of your time to optimize against the cost of the service. When you pay for *Listings* or *Spidering*, you have no guarantee of ranks.

Ranks:

There are several search engines that now charge for ranks. You bid on keywords and you are placed in the list based on your bid. To find articles listing the search engines that do this and more, relative to how the process works, go to the Online Tutorial and look for the article, "Paying For Ranks, Listings, and Spidering."

Listings:

You definitely want to consider paying for listings in the major online directories if you can't get in for free. A few of the online directories no longer allow free submissions. You will need to pay for a review for any hope of being listed. Each directory has its own guidelines for paying. You will find information on each particular directory at:

www.thewritemarket.com/directories.shtml

Spidering:

During the writing of this booklet, Inktomi is the only engine with a "Pay for Spidering" model. This takes the mystery out of wondering when the search engine's spider will come to your site and grab your changes. It's important to realize that in this model, there is no guarantee of rank, only a guarantee that the spider will visit the page that you've paid for.

More information will be available in the Online Tutorial under "Paying For Ranks, Listings, and Spidering."

Paid Ranking

Paid Listings

Paid Spidering

UPDATING

Promotion in the search engines and directories is all about content.

Developing content will consist of two things:

1. Optimizing web pages for the SEs (working on the title, description and keyword frequency in the text)
2. Adding new pages or new updates to support your current information.

Updating will keep your web site fresh and help you get *repeat* visitors.

Develop a plan to update:

1. Set aside a few hours on a regular schedule to work on content (like once a week).
2. Write down a list of the content you intend to work on.
3. Write down a tentative start date (the day that you intend to work on the specific task.)
4. Write down when you complete the task.

The next few pages will help you develop your update plan...

Content Update Schedule

Content	Date to Start	Date Finished

Content Update Schedule

Content	Date to Start	Date Finished

Content Update Schedule

Content	Date to Start	Date Finished

CONCLUSION

Thank you for reading. If you have any questions, comments, or critiques please send them to:

Webmaster@thewritemarket.com

The Write Market

RR1 Box 130M

Shenandoah Junction, WV 25442

Websites to remember:

Software to consider:

Contacts:

Discussion Boards/Forums:

Notes

Printed in the United States
6168